KIDS TRAVEL GUIDE TO SCOTLAND

Discover The Ultimate Trip Guide To Scottish Most Beautiful Landscapes With Their Culture History And Attraction

Sarah Wiseman

Copyright ©Sarah Wiseman

All rights reserved. No part of this book may be reproduced in any form or by any electronic or mechanical means, including information storage and retrieval systems, without permission in writing from the publisher, except by a reviewer who may quote brief passages in a review.

TABLE OF CONTENT

INTRODUCTION...................................6

About This Book...........................8

How to Use This Guide 9

CHAPTER 1..............................11

Getting Ready for Your Trip...............12

Planning Your Trip to Scotland 12

Packing Essentials for Kids...............17

Learning About Scotland's Culture
and History............................20

CHAPTER 2.............................24

Welcome to Scotland!......................24

Arrival in Scotland 24

Scotland at a Glance 27

Famous Scottish Landmarks 30

Fun Facts about Scotland 33

CHAPTER 3 36

Exploring Scottish Cities 36

Edinburgh 36

Glasgow 42

Inverness 47

CHAPTER 4 51

Discovering Scottish Nature 52

Scottish Highlands 52

Lochs and Islands 56

Highland Cows 60

CHAPTER 5 64

Uncovering Scottish History and Legends 64

Ancient Scotland 64

Scottish Myths and Legends 68

CHAPTER 6 73

Scottish Traditions and Festivals 74

Tartan and Kilts................................ 74

Highland Games 77

Hogmanay (New Year's Eve) Celebrations 80

The Edinburgh Festival Fringe......... 83

CHAPTER 7 86

Tasting Scotland 88

Traditional Scottish Food.................. 88

Trying Scottish Whisky (for the parents!) 91

CHAPTER 8 94

Fun Activities for Kids 94

CHAPTER 9 98

Helpful Phrases and Glossary 98

CONCLUSION 100

INTRODUCTION

Seven years ago, I embarked on a life-changing journey with my children to the enchanting land of Scotland. It was a trip filled with anticipation and excitement, as we eagerly set foot on this land of ancient castles, rugged landscapes, and rich traditions. Little did I know that this extraordinary vacation would not only create indelible memories but also inspire me to share our experiences through the creation of the Kids Travel Guide to Scotland.

From the moment we arrived, Scotland embraced us with open arms. The warmth and friendliness of the Scottish people made us feel instantly at home. Their genuine smiles and willingness to share their stories and traditions created a sense of belonging that we carried with us throughout our adventure.

Our days were filled with awe-inspiring experiences. We explored the historic streets of Edinburgh, where the grandeur of Edinburgh Castle left us speechless. We marveled at the striking beauty of Loch Ness, hoping to catch a glimpse of the legendary Nessie. The Scottish Highlands beckoned us with their majestic mountains and shimmering lochs, inviting us to embark on breathtaking hikes and discover hidden gems at every turn.

Immersing ourselves in Scottish culture, we attended the vibrant Edinburgh Festival Fringe, where the streets came alive with performers, musicians, and laughter. We savored the delectable flavors of traditional Scottish food, from hearty haggis to buttery shortbread, delighting our taste buds with each bite.

But it was the people we met along the way who truly made this journey unforgettable. From the passionate storytellers who transported us to mythical worlds, to the kind-hearted locals who shared their knowledge and hospitality, Scotland's people left an indelible mark on our hearts. Their warmth and genuine connection reminded us of the power of human connection and the beauty of cultural exchange.

As the days turned into cherished memories, I realized the profound impact this journey had on my children and myself. Their curious minds were ignited, their perspectives broadened, and their appreciation for different cultures deepened. And it was in that moment of reflection that the idea of the Kids Travel Guide to Scotland was born.

Through the pages of the guide, I aimed to capture the essence of our unforgettable experiences. I wanted to share the beauty of Scotland with other children, inspiring them to explore, learn, and embrace the wonders of this extraordinary country. I wanted to ignite their sense of adventure and instill in them a deep appreciation for the diversity and magic that travel brings.

Scotland had become more than just a destination; it had become a part of our story. Its landscapes, its people, its rich history had woven themselves into the fabric of our lives. And as I poured my heart and soul into the creation of the Kids Travel Guide to Scotland, I knew that our incredible journey would continue to live on through the words and experiences shared with young travelers around the world.

Scotland had gifted us with unforgettable memories, a sense of wonder, and a burning desire to explore further. It had given us the courage to follow our passions and share our stories. And as we look back on that life-changing vacation, we are forever grateful for the beauty, the joy, and the inspiration that Scotland bestowed upon us.

About This Book

The Kids Travel Guide to Scotland is an exciting and informative resource designed specifically for young travelers who are planning to visit Scotland. This book aims to make the journey to Scotland an unforgettable adventure for children, filled with fascinating information about the country's history, culture, landmarks, nature, and traditions.

This guidebook is written in a child-friendly language, making it easy for young readers to understand and engage with the content.

It presents the information in an engaging and interactive format, incorporating fun facts, colorful illustrations, maps, and activities that will keep children entertained throughout their Scottish journey.

The book covers a wide range of topics, including Scottish cities, famous landmarks, natural wonders, Scottish history and legends, traditional festivals, local cuisine, and much more. It provides a comprehensive overview of Scotland, allowing young travelers to gain a deeper understanding of the country's unique heritage and its vibrant culture.

How to Use This Guide

The Kids Travel Guide to Scotland is designed to be user-friendly and interactive, making it easy for children to navigate and explore the content. Here's a brief guide on how to make the most of this book:

a) Begin with the Introduction: Start by reading the introduction section, which gives a warm welcome to Scotland and provides an overview of what to expect from the book. This section will get young travelers excited about their upcoming adventure.

b) Plan Your Trip: In the "Getting Ready for Your Trip" chapter, children will find valuable information on planning their trip to

Scotland. They will learn about the best time to visit, what to pack, and how to prepare themselves for an amazing journey.

c) Explore Different Sections: The book is divided into several sections, each focusing on a specific aspect of Scotland. Children can explore chapters dedicated to Scottish cities, famous landmarks, nature, history, traditions, and more. They can read through each chapter in sequence or jump to the sections that interest them the most.

d) Engage with Activities: Throughout the book, there are interactive activities, puzzles, and quizzes that will allow children to actively participate in their learning. These activities are designed to be educational and entertaining, enhancing the overall experience of discovering Scotland.

e) Discover Fun Facts: The Kids Travel Guide to Scotland is filled with intriguing facts about the country. Encourage children to explore the "Fun Facts" sections scattered throughout the book to expand their knowledge and impress their friends and family with interesting Scottish trivia.

f) Use the Maps: The appendix of the book includes maps of Scotland, helping young travelers to locate cities, landmarks, and other points of interest. The maps are labeled with key attractions, making it easier for children to plan their itinerary and navigate their way around the country.

g) Learn Useful Phrases: Towards the end of the book, there is a section dedicated to useful Scottish phrases. Encourage children to practice these phrases and embrace the local language, adding a fun and interactive element to their journey.

By following these tips, young travelers can maximize their experience with the Kids Travel Guide to Scotland, immersing themselves in the wonders of this beautiful country and creating lasting memories of their Scottish adventure.

CHAPTER 1

Getting Ready for Your Trip

Planning Your Trip to Scotland

Planning a trip to Scotland can be an exciting and rewarding experience, especially when traveling with children. To guarantee a smooth and comfortable trip, it's important to take a number of elements into account. In this section, we will explore important aspects to keep in mind when planning your trip to Scotland with the help of the Kids Travel Guide to Scotland.

Best Time to Visit:

When deciding on the best time to visit Scotland, it's important to consider the weather, school holidays, and the activities and attractions you wish to experience. Scotland has a temperate maritime climate, which means it can be unpredictable throughout the year. The summer months (June to August) generally offer milder weather and longer daylight hours, making it an ideal time for outdoor adventures. However, it's worth noting that these months are also peak tourist season. Spring (March to May) and autumn (September to November) can provide pleasant weather with fewer crowds. Winter (December to February) offers a unique charm, especially for those interested in winter sports or witnessing the stunning landscapes covered in snow.

Duration of Stay:

The Kids Travel Guide to Scotland suggests allocating sufficient time to explore the country thoroughly. Scotland offers a diverse range of experiences, from vibrant cities to breathtaking landscapes, and each region has its own unique attractions. Depending on your interests, consider spending at least a week or two to truly immerse yourself in Scotland's beauty and culture. This will allow you to visit major cities like Edinburgh and Glasgow, explore the stunning Highlands, discover historical sites, and indulge in outdoor activities.

Choosing Accommodation:

Scotland offers a wide range of accommodation options suitable for families, including hotels, guesthouses, self-catering cottages, and even castle stays. When traveling with children, it's essential to select accommodation that caters to their needs. Look for family-friendly establishments that provide amenities like spacious rooms, play areas, and child-friendly dining options. Additionally, consider the location of your accommodation, ensuring it is convenient for exploring the attractions and has access to public transportation.

[13]

Transportation:

Getting around Scotland can be an adventure in itself. The Kids Travel Guide to Scotland suggests considering different transportation options based on your itinerary and preferences. Scotland has an extensive network of trains, buses, and ferries, making it relatively easy to navigate between cities and regions. Trains are a convenient and scenic mode of transportation, especially when traveling longer distances. Buses offer flexibility and access to remote areas. If you plan to explore the islands, ferries are often the primary means of transportation. Car rental is also a popular choice, providing freedom and flexibility to explore at your own pace. Ensure you have appropriate car seats and follow safety guidelines when traveling with young children.

Research and Itinerary Planning:

To make the most of your trip, it's recommended to research Scotland's attractions, activities, and events in advance. The Kids Travel Guide to Scotland offers insights into popular landmarks, historical sites, natural wonders, festivals, and more. Take the time to create a flexible itinerary that includes a mix of city exploration, outdoor adventures, cultural experiences, and time for relaxation. Involving children in the planning process can be fun and educational, allowing them to learn about Scotland's history and culture while choosing activities that interest them.

[14]

Safety and Health:

Your family should always come first, both in terms of safety and well-being. Before traveling to Scotland, ensure you have travel insurance that covers medical emergencies. Familiarize yourself with basic safety guidelines and emergency contact numbers. It's also advisable to carry necessary medications, a first aid kit, and any specific items your children may require. Scotland is generally a safe destination, but it's important to practice general safety precautions, such as keeping an eye on personal belongings and staying together as a group in crowded areas.

Travel Documents and Entry Requirements:

Before traveling to Scotland, make sure to check the passport and visa requirements for your country of residence. Ensure that all family members have valid passports with sufficient validity for the duration of your stay. Depending on your nationality, you may require a visa to enter Scotland or the United Kingdom. It's essential to check the official government websites or consult with the relevant embassy or consulate to confirm the entry requirements well in advance of your trip.

Budgeting:

Scotland can offer a range of options for different budgets. It's important to establish a budget for your trip and consider factors such as accommodation, transportation, meals, activities, and souvenirs. The Kids Travel Guide to Scotland can provide insights into affordable or free attractions and activities suitable for families. Researching and pre-booking certain attractions or accommodations can help you secure the best deals and manage your expenses effectively.

Special Considerations for Kids:

When planning a trip to Scotland with children, it's crucial to consider their interests, energy levels, and needs. Ensure that your itinerary includes a balance of activities suitable for all ages. Look for child-friendly attractions, parks, and interactive museums that offer educational and entertaining experiences. Allow for breaks and downtime during the day to avoid overexertion. Packing essentials such as snacks, water bottles, comfortable clothing, and weather-appropriate gear will contribute to a smoother and more enjoyable trip for the whole family.

By taking into account these planning considerations and using the Kids Travel Guide to Scotland as a valuable resource, you can create a well-organized and memorable trip that caters to the interests and needs of your family. Remember to embrace the spirit of adventure, have fun, and create lasting memories of your Scottish journey.

Packing Essentials for Kids

When preparing for a trip to Scotland with children, packing the right essentials is crucial to ensure their comfort, safety, and enjoyment throughout the journey. The Kids Travel Guide to Scotland provides valuable insights into the items that are essential for a successful and hassle-free adventure. Here are some key packing essentials for kids when traveling to Scotland:

Clothing:

Layered Clothing: Scotland's weather can be unpredictable, so packing layers is essential. Include items such as t-shirts, long-sleeved shirts, sweaters, and a lightweight jacket or raincoat. This will allow children to adjust their clothing according to the changing weather conditions.

Waterproof Outerwear: Scotland is known for its occasional rain showers, so pack a waterproof jacket or poncho to keep kids dry and comfortable during outdoor activities.

Comfortable Shoes: Scotland offers a variety of terrains, from city streets to rugged landscapes. Pack comfortable and sturdy shoes for walking and exploring. If you plan to hike or explore nature trails, consider packing waterproof and durable footwear.

Travel Accessories:

Daypack or Backpack: A small daypack or backpack for each child is essential for carrying snacks, water bottles, extra clothing layers, and personal belongings during day trips and excursions.

Travel Documents: Ensure that each child has their passport, identification, and any necessary travel documents stored in a safe and easily accessible place.

Money and Small Wallet: If children will be responsible for their own spending, provide them with a small wallet or pouch to keep their money secure.

Travel Games and Activities: Keep children entertained during travel by packing small games, books, coloring materials, or electronic devices with headphones.

Health and Safety:

Medications and First Aid Kit: Pack any necessary medications for your children, including prescription drugs, allergy medication, and pain relievers. Additionally, carry a basic first aid kit with band-aids, antiseptic ointment, and any specific items your child may require.

Hand Sanitizer and Wipes: Maintain good hygiene by carrying hand sanitizer and antibacterial wipes to clean hands and surfaces during the trip.

Sun Protection: Even on cloudy days, UV rays can be strong in Scotland. Pack sunscreen, sunglasses, and hats to protect children's skin and eyes.

Insect Repellent: If you plan to spend time outdoors, particularly in rural areas, packing insect repellent can help protect children from bug bites.

Entertainment and Comfort:

Snacks and Water Bottles: Carry a supply of healthy snacks and reusable water bottles to keep children nourished and hydrated throughout the trip.

Comfort Items: If your child has a favorite stuffed animal, blanket, or pillow, pack these familiar comfort items to help them feel secure and at ease during travel and accommodation.

Miscellaneous:

Adapters and Chargers: If you plan to use electronic devices, ensure you have the appropriate adapters and chargers for Scotland's power outlets.

Language Guide: Consider packing a pocket-sized language guide or phrasebook that includes basic Scottish phrases. This can be a fun way for children to learn and engage with the local culture.

It's important to involve children in the packing process, allowing them to contribute and understand what is necessary for their trip. Encourage them to pack their own bags (with supervision) to develop a sense of responsibility and independence.

By considering these packing essentials outlined in the Kids Travel Guide to Scotland, you can ensure that your children are well-prepared for the Scottish adventure, allowing them to enjoy the journey comfortably and with excitement.

Learning About Scotland's Culture and History

Understanding Scotland's culture and history is a key aspect of immersing oneself in the country's rich heritage. The Kids Travel Guide to Scotland offers a variety of engaging ways for children to learn about Scotland's culture and history, providing a deeper appreciation for the places they will visit. Here are several intriguing angles to investigate:

<u>Scottish Traditions and Customs</u>:

[20]

Introduce children to Scottish traditions and customs that make the country unique. Topics to explore may include:

Tartan and Kilts: Explain the significance of tartan patterns and the traditional Scottish garment known as the kilt.

Bagpipes and Music: Explore the distinctive sounds of bagpipes, a traditional Scottish musical instrument, and the importance of music in Scottish culture.

Ceilidh Dancing: Teach children about traditional Scottish dances, such as the ceilidh, and encourage them to try some basic dance steps.

Scottish Food: Introduce children to traditional Scottish cuisine, such as haggis, shortbread, and cranachan, and explain their cultural significance.

Scottish History:

Scotland has a fascinating history that spans thousands of years. The Kids Travel Guide to Scotland can provide an overview of significant historical events and figures. Some key topics to explore may include:

Ancient Scotland: Learn about ancient Scottish history, including topics such as Celtic tribes, Roman influence, and the Picts.

Castles and Battlefields: Discover the stories behind Scotland's iconic castles, such as Edinburgh Castle and Stirling Castle, and famous battlefields like Culloden Battlefield.

The Jacobites: Explore the Jacobite rebellions and the struggle for Scottish independence, including the story of Bonnie Prince Charlie.

Mary, Queen of Scots: Learn about the life and reign of Mary, Queen of Scots, and her impact on Scottish history.

Scottish Legends and Myths:

Scotland is renowned for its captivating legends and myths that have been passed down through generations. Engage children with these enchanting tales, such as:

The Loch Ness Monster: Uncover the legend of the Loch Ness Monster, known as "Nessie," and the mysteries surrounding Loch Ness.

The Legend of Braveheart: Explore the story of William Wallace, a Scottish hero, and his fight for independence, popularized in the movie "Braveheart."

The Fairy Pools: Discover the magical Fairy Pools on the Isle of Skye and the stories of fairies and mystical creatures in Scottish folklore.

Scottish Language and Phrases:

Introduce children to basic Scottish phrases and words to foster an appreciation for the local language. The Kids Travel Guide to Scotland can include a section dedicated to useful Scottish phrases and their pronunciation. Teach them greetings, common expressions, and simple phrases to engage with locals and enhance their cultural experience.

Encourage children to actively participate in learning about Scotland's culture and history by incorporating interactive activities and games into the learning process. This can include quizzes, puzzles, and creative projects that allow them to explore and showcase their knowledge.

By delving into Scotland's culture and history with the Kids Travel Guide to Scotland, children can develop a deeper understanding of the country's unique identity and appreciate the significance of the places they visit. It will enhance their overall experience and create lasting memories of their Scottish adventure.

CHAPTER 2

Welcome to Scotland!

Arrival in Scotland

The arrival in Scotland marks the beginning of an exciting adventure for children exploring the country. The Kids Travel Guide to Scotland provides valuable information to help make the arrival experience smooth and enjoyable. Here's a detailed explanation of what children can expect upon their arrival in Scotland:

Airport or Port Arrival:

a) Flights: If arriving by air, children will disembark at one of Scotland's major airports, such as Edinburgh Airport, Glasgow Airport, or Aberdeen Airport. They will follow the signs to immigration and customs, where passports and travel documents will be checked. The Kids Travel Guide to Scotland can explain the process, reassuring children about the necessary procedures.

b) Ferries: For those arriving by ferry, such as from Northern Ireland or the Orkney Islands, children will disembark at the designated port. They can expect to follow signs to immigration or passport control, if applicable.

Immigration and Customs:

Upon arrival, children will encounter immigration and customs procedures. The Kids Travel Guide to Scotland can provide a brief explanation of these processes, including the importance of presenting valid travel documents and complying with customs regulations. Encourage children to remain patient and follow the instructions of airport or port staff.

Baggage Claim:

After passing through immigration, children will proceed to the baggage claim area. Here, they will locate the designated conveyor belts or collection points to retrieve their checked luggage. It is essential to remind children to identify their bags properly and ensure they collect their own belongings.

Transportation Options:

Once children have collected their luggage, they can explore transportation options to reach their accommodation or continue their journey. Scotland offers various transportation modes:

a) Taxis: Taxis are readily available outside airports and ports, providing a convenient and direct means of transportation. The Kids Travel Guide to Scotland can explain the process of locating and hiring a taxi.

[25]

b) Public Transportation: Scotland has an extensive public transportation network, including buses, trains, and trams. Children can learn about the availability of public transportation and how to navigate the system using maps and schedules.

c) Car Rental: Families who prefer the flexibility of having their own vehicle can opt for car rental services. The Kids Travel Guide to Scotland can explain the process of renting a car, including necessary documentation and safety precautions.

Currency Exchange and Money Matters:

Children may need to exchange currency upon arrival in Scotland. The Kids Travel Guide to Scotland can provide information about currency exchange services, their locations, and the importance of exchanging money at reputable establishments. It can also explain the use of ATMs and credit cards for financial transactions.

Language and Communication:

Scotland's official language is English, but there are regional accents and dialects to be aware of. The Kids Travel Guide to Scotland can introduce children to basic Scottish phrases and encourage them to practice greetings and simple conversational phrases. This can help them feel more comfortable communicating with locals and immersing themselves in the local culture.

Welcome to Scotland:

Children should be reminded that their arrival in Scotland marks the beginning of an exciting adventure. The Kids Travel Guide to Scotland can provide a warm welcome, highlighting the country's unique features, such as its breathtaking landscapes, rich history, and friendly people. Encourage children to embrace the experience with enthusiasm and curiosity.

By providing children with a detailed understanding of what to expect upon arrival in Scotland, as outlined in the Kids Travel Guide to Scotland, their arrival experience can be seamless and filled with anticipation for the adventures that lie ahead.

Scotland at a Glance

Scotland is a fascinating country with a diverse range of attractions and experiences to offer young travelers. The Kids Travel Guide to Scotland provides a concise overview of Scotland at a glance, helping children understand the country's unique characteristics and highlights. Here's a detailed explanation of what children can learn about Scotland at a glance:

Geography and Landscapes:

Introduce children to Scotland's geography and its stunning landscapes. Scotland is located in the northern part of the United

Kingdom and shares borders with England to the south. The country is known for its breathtaking landscapes, including mountains, lochs (lakes), rivers, and picturesque coastlines. The Kids Travel Guide to Scotland can showcase images and describe the different geographical features, such as the Scottish Highlands, the Isle of Skye, and the famous Loch Ness.

Capital City and Major Cities:

The Kids Travel Guide to Scotland can provide an overview of Scotland's capital city, Edinburgh, as well as other major cities such as Glasgow, Inverness, and Aberdeen. Children can learn about the unique characteristics and attractions of each city. For example:

Edinburgh: Highlight the iconic Edinburgh Castle, the Royal Mile, and the city's rich history.

Glasgow: Emphasize its vibrant art and music scene, museums, and distinctive architecture.

Inverness: Discuss the city's location as the gateway to the Scottish Highlands and its proximity to Loch Ness.

Aberdeen: Mention its importance as a hub for the oil and gas industry and its stunning sandy beaches.

Famous Scottish Landmarks:

Introduce children to some of Scotland's most famous landmarks that they may encounter during their journey. The Kids Travel Guide to Scotland can feature descriptions and illustrations of these landmarks, including:

Edinburgh Castle: Explain the history and significance of Edinburgh Castle, located atop Castle Rock in the heart of the city.

Loch Ness: Capture children's imagination with the legendary Loch Ness and the story of the Loch Ness Monster, affectionately known as Nessie.

The Isle of Skye: Highlight the Isle of Skye's rugged landscapes, including the Fairy Pools, the Old Man of Storr, and its connection to Scottish folklore.

Scottish Wildlife:

Scotland is home to a variety of unique wildlife. The Kids Travel Guide to Scotland can introduce children to some of these fascinating creatures, such as:

Highland Cows: Describe the distinctive appearance of Highland cows (also known as "coos") with their long horns and shaggy hair.

Red Deer: Teach children about red deer, the largest land mammal in the country, and their natural habitats.

Puffins: Spark children's interest in puffins, adorable seabirds that inhabit Scotland's coastal regions during certain times of the year.

Fun Facts about Scotland:

To pique children's curiosity, the Kids Travel Guide to Scotland can include fun facts and trivia about the country. These may include interesting tidbits about Scottish inventions (such as the telephone and television), famous Scots (like Sir Walter Scott and Alexander Graham Bell), and cultural traditions (such as Highland games and the Scottish kilt). Fun facts can engage children and encourage them to share their newfound knowledge with family and friends.

By providing children with a snapshot of Scotland at a glance, as outlined in the Kids Travel Guide to Scotland, they can gain a better understanding of the country's geography, major cities, famous landmarks, wildlife, and unique cultural aspects. This knowledge will enrich their overall travel experience and deepen their appreciation for Scotland's beauty and heritage.

Famous Scottish Landmarks

Scotland is renowned for its iconic landmarks that capture the imagination and awe of visitors of all ages. The Kids Travel Guide to Scotland showcases these famous landmarks, providing children with a deeper understanding of their historical and cultural significance. Here's a detailed explanation of some of Scotland's most famous landmarks that children can discover:

Edinburgh Castle:

Edinburgh Castle is an iconic symbol of Scotland and a must-visit landmark in the capital city. Children can learn about its fascinating history, from its origins as a fortress to its transformation into a royal palace and military stronghold. The Kids Travel Guide to Scotland can describe the grandeur of the castle's architecture, the stories of its former residents, and the breathtaking views of the city from its ramparts. Encourage children to imagine themselves as knights or princesses as they explore the castle's various sections, including the Crown Jewels, the Great Hall, and the eerie dungeons.

The Isle of Skye:

The Kids Travel Guide to Scotland can transport children to the rugged and picturesque landscapes of the Isle of Skye. They can explore the famous landmarks that make this island a captivating destination. Highlight the Fairy Pools, a series of crystal-clear, blue-hued pools and waterfalls that seem straight out of a fairytale. Describe the unique rock formations of the Old Man of Storr, standing tall and mysterious against the backdrop of dramatic cliffs. Additionally, mention the Quiraing, a geological marvel

[31]

with its stunning cliffs and sweeping vistas. These landmarks provide children with a sense of wonder and appreciation for Scotland's natural beauty.

Other Notable Landmarks:

There are many other notable landmarks in Scotland that children can discover through the Kids Travel Guide to Scotland. These may include:

Stirling Castle: Teach children about Stirling Castle, an impressive fortress perched high on a hill with breathtaking views. Describe its role in Scottish history, including its connection to William Wallace and the Wars of Independence.

Eilean Donan Castle: Introduce children to the iconic Eilean Donan Castle, situated on a small island at the meeting point of three lochs. Highlight its picturesque setting and the stunning views of the castle against the backdrop of the Scottish Highlands.

The Kelpies: Spark children's interest in the monumental sculptures known as The Kelpies. These towering horse head sculptures celebrate Scotland's equine heritage and mythology.

Encourage children to imagine themselves stepping into the pages of history or mythical tales as they explore these famous landmarks. The Kids Travel Guide to Scotland can provide

[32]

fascinating details, captivating illustrations, and anecdotes that bring these landmarks to life, fostering a sense of adventure and curiosity.

Fun Facts about Scotland

Scotland is a country filled with interesting and fun facts that can capture the imagination of young travelers. The Kids Travel Guide to Scotland can introduce children to these delightful tidbits, sparking their curiosity and making their Scottish adventure even more exciting. Here are some engaging fun facts about Scotland:

Inventions and Discoveries:

Scotland has been the birthplace of many remarkable inventions and discoveries. The Kids Travel Guide to Scotland can highlight a few, such as:

The Telephone: Share the story of Alexander Graham Bell, a Scottish scientist credited with inventing the telephone.

Television: Explain that John Logie Baird, a Scottish engineer, played a crucial role in the development of television technology.

Penicillin: Discuss how Scottish scientist Alexander Fleming discovered penicillin, an antibiotic that revolutionized medicine.

Highland Games:

Scotland is famous for its Highland Games, where athletes compete in traditional Scottish sports. The Kids Travel Guide to Scotland can explain that these games feature events such as caber tossing (tossing a large wooden pole), hammer throwing, and tug-of-war. Children can learn about the excitement and festive atmosphere of these traditional sporting events.

Traditional Scottish Clothing:

Introduce children to traditional Scottish clothing, such as the kilt and tartan. The Kids Travel Guide to Scotland can explain that tartan is a pattern of crisscrossing colored stripes that represents different Scottish clans and families. Children can learn about the significance of tartan and how kilts are worn for special occasions like weddings and celebrations.

Fairy Pools and Fairy Folklore:

Scotland is rich in folklore and mythical tales, including stories of fairies. The Kids Travel Guide to Scotland can introduce children to the enchanting Fairy Pools on the Isle of Skye. Explain the magical allure of these crystal-clear pools and their connection to Scottish fairy folklore. Children can let their imaginations soar as they explore these mystical landscapes.

Scottish Wildlife:

Scotland is home to unique and fascinating wildlife. The Kids Travel Guide to Scotland can highlight some of these creatures, such as:

Highland Cows (Coos): Describe the distinctive appearance of these shaggy-haired cows with their long horns, often seen grazing in the Scottish Highlands.

Red Deer: Share interesting facts about the red deer, Scotland's largest land mammal, and its natural habitats.

Puffins: Spark children's interest in puffins, adorable seabirds that inhabit Scotland's coastal regions during certain times of the year.

Traditional Scottish Music and Dance:

Scotland is renowned for its lively traditional music and energetic dancing. The Kids Travel Guide to Scotland can introduce children to Scottish music instruments like the bagpipes and the fiddle. Children can learn about the unique rhythms and melodies of Scottish music and discover the joy of traditional Scottish dancing, such as the ceilidh.

Encourage children to share these fun facts with their family and friends, allowing them to become young ambassadors of Scottish culture and knowledge. By incorporating these engaging facts into the Kids Travel Guide to Scotland, children will develop a deeper appreciation for the country's heritage, traditions, and natural wonders.

CHAPTER 3

Exploring Scottish Cities

Edinburgh

Edinburgh, the capital city of Scotland, is a captivating destination that offers a wealth of experiences for young travelers. From its historic landmarks to its vibrant cultural scene, Edinburgh has something to delight children of all ages. The Kids Travel Guide to Scotland can serve as an excellent resource to help children explore and appreciate the wonders of Edinburgh. Here's a long, detailed explanation of what children can discover while exploring the city:

Edinburgh Castle:

A visit to Edinburgh would not be complete without exploring Edinburgh Castle, a magnificent fortress that sits atop Castle Rock. The Kids Travel Guide to Scotland can provide fascinating details about the castle's history, such as its origins as a royal residence and its role as a military stronghold. Children can embark on an adventure through the castle's various sections, including the Crown Jewels, the Great Hall, and the Stone of Destiny. Encourage them to imagine themselves as knights or princesses as they walk through the castle's grand courtyards and learn about its captivating stories.

Royal Mile:

The Royal Mile is a historic street that stretches between Edinburgh Castle and the Palace of Holyroodhouse. Children can immerse themselves in the medieval atmosphere as they explore this bustling thoroughfare. The Kids Travel Guide to Scotland can guide children through the Royal Mile, pointing out notable landmarks such as St. Giles' Cathedral, John Knox House, and the Writers' Museum. They can discover unique shops, street performers, and charming narrow closes (alleyways) along this iconic street. Encourage children to keep an eye out for the Heart of Midlothian, a heart-shaped mosaic on the pavement, and join the tradition of giving it a good luck touch or spit.

Palace of Holyroodhouse:

Located at the end of the Royal Mile, the Palace of Holyroodhouse is the official residence of the British monarch in Scotland. The Kids Travel Guide to Scotland can introduce children to the palace's rich history and notable features, such as the State Apartments and the ruins of Holyrood Abbey. They can learn about its connections to Scottish royalty and explore the beautiful

[37]

gardens surrounding the palace. Children might even spot the Queen's Gallery, which showcases art from the Royal Collection.

Dynamic Earth:

Visitors to the interactive science museum Dynamic Earth are taken on a tour through the Earth's past.. The Kids Travel Guide to Scotland can describe the engaging exhibits and activities that allow children to explore topics such as dinosaurs, earthquakes, and the formation of landscapes. They can participate in hands-on experiments and simulations that make learning about Earth's natural processes exciting and educational. From walking through a prehistoric forest to experiencing a polar expedition, Dynamic Earth offers a dynamic learning experience.

Arthur's Seat and Holyrood Park:

Arthur's Seat is an ancient volcano that forms part of Holyrood Park, a vast green space located near the Palace of Holyroodhouse. The Kids Travel Guide to Scotland can guide children on a hike up Arthur's Seat, highlighting the panoramic views of the city and the surrounding landscapes. They can learn about the volcanic origins of the hill and the diverse flora and fauna found in the park. Encourage children to bring their cameras to capture the stunning vistas from the summit and enjoy a picnic or a game in the park's open spaces.

[38]

Camera Obscura and World of Illusions:

The Camera Obscura and World of Illusions is a unique attraction that offers a blend of optical illusions, interactive exhibits, and panoramic views of Edinburgh. The Kids Travel Guide to Scotland can explain the fascinating world of illusions, where children can experience mind-boggling visual effects and participate in hands-on activities. They can explore the rooftop terrace for captivating views of the city and engage in the wonders of perception and perspective. From distorting mirrors to holograms andholographic displays, the Camera Obscura and World of Illusions provide a fun and educational experience.

Museums and Galleries:

Edinburgh is home to numerous museums and galleries that cater to a variety of interests. The Kids Travel Guide to Scotland can highlight specific venues suitable for children, such as the National Museum of Scotland, the Museum of Edinburgh, and the Scottish National Gallery of Modern Art. Children can learn about Scotland's history, culture, and art through interactive displays, artifacts, and engaging exhibits designed for young minds. From discovering the secrets of dinosaurs to exploring Scottish art and design, these museums and galleries offer a wealth of knowledge and inspiration.

The Real Mary King's Close:

The Real Mary King's Close is an underground tour that takes children on a fascinating journey through the hidden streets and spaces beneath the Royal Mile. The Kids Travel Guide to Scotland can describe the history and legends associated with this mysterious underground labyrinth. Children can explore the reconstructed rooms and hear stories of the people who once lived there, offering a glimpse into Edinburgh's past.

Scottish Storytelling Centre:

The Scottish Storytelling Centre is dedicated to preserving and celebrating Scotland's rich oral tradition. The Kids Travel Guide to Scotland can introduce children to the art of storytelling through workshops and performances. They can listen to captivating tales of Scottish myths, legends, and folklore, sparking their imagination and connecting them to the country's cultural heritage.

Calton Hill:

Calton Hill is a prominent hill located in the heart of Edinburgh, offering panoramic views of the city. The Kids Travel Guide to Scotland can highlight the impressive monuments and structures found on Calton Hill, such as the National Monument, the Nelson Monument, and the City Observatory. Children can climb to the top of the hill and enjoy the breathtaking vistas, capturing memorable photos of the cityscape and landmarks.

The Edinburgh Festival:

If visiting during the summer, children can experience the world-famous Edinburgh Festival, which includes various events such as the Edinburgh Festival Fringe, the Edinburgh International Festival, and the Royal Edinburgh Military Tattoo. The Kids Travel Guide to Scotland can explain the festival's vibrant atmosphere, with street performances, theater shows, music concerts, and more. Children can participate in family-friendly events and soak up the creative energy that fills the city during this time.

Scottish Food and Treats:

The Kids Travel Guide to Scotland can introduce children to traditional Scottish cuisine and treats. They can discover the delights of Scottish shortbread, try haggis (a savory dish made with sheep's heart, liver, and lungs), and sample Scottish tablet (a sweet confection made from sugar, butter, and condensed milk). Children can embrace the culinary traditions of Scotland and develop a taste for its unique flavors.

Encourage children to embrace the spirit of exploration as they venture through Edinburgh with the Kids Travel Guide to

Scotland. Let them take the lead in choosing attractions and activities that capture their interest, allowing them to immerse themselves in the city's history, culture, and natural beauty. Edinburgh offers an abundance of enriching experiences that will create lasting memories of their Scottish journey.

Glasgow

Glasgow, the largest city in Scotland, is a vibrant and cultural hub with a wealth of attractions for young travelers to explore. The Kids Travel Guide to Scotland can serve as an excellent resource to help children discover the wonders of Glasgow. Here's a detailed explanation of what children can experience while exploring the city:

Kelvingrove Art Gallery and Museum:

The Kids Travel Guide to Scotland can introduce children to the Kelvingrove Art Gallery and Museum, a fascinating venue that offers a diverse range of exhibits. Children can explore the museum's collections, which include art, natural history, and ancient artifacts. They can discover the famous Spitfire plane, marvel at the exhibits on dinosaurs and animals, and admire the stunning artwork on display. Encourage children to engage with interactive displays and participate in any educational programs or workshops offered.

Glasgow Science Centre:

The Glasgow Science Centre is an interactive science museum that provides a hands-on learning experience for children. The Kids Travel Guide to Scotland can describe the exciting exhibits and activities available, such as the Science Mall, the Planetarium, and the IMAX cinema. Children can participate in interactive experiments, learn about space and the universe, and enjoy thrilling science shows. The Science Centre offers a fun and educational environment that sparks curiosity and encourages a love for science.

Riverside Museum:

The Kids Travel Guide to Scotland can introduce children to the Riverside Museum, a captivating museum dedicated to transportation and Glasgow's history. Children can explore the vast collection of vintage cars, bicycles, and locomotives. They can step aboard a real steam locomotive, interact with interactive displays, and learn about the evolution of transportation over the years. The museum also houses a recreation of a typical Glasgow street from the early 20th century, providing a glimpse into the city's past.

Glasgow Cathedral:

Glasgow Cathedral, also known as St. Mungo's Cathedral, is a magnificent medieval building with a rich history. The Kids Travel

Guide to Scotland can explain the significance of the cathedral and its stunning architectural features, such as the stained glass windows and the intricate stone carvings. Children can explore the interior of the cathedral, learn about its role in Scottish history, and discover the stories of Saint Mungo, the patron saint of Glasgow.

Glasgow Botanic Gardens:

The Glasgow Botanic Gardens offer a peaceful escape from the bustling city. The Kids Travel Guide to Scotland can describe the beautiful gardens, including the Kibble Palace, a glasshouse filled with exotic plants and sculptures. Children can wander through the various gardens, learn about different plant species, and enjoy the tranquility of nature. The Botanic Gardens also host special events and workshops for children, providing an opportunity to engage with nature in a fun and educational way.

People's Palace and Winter Gardens:

The People's Palace and Winter Gardens is a cultural museum that offers insight into the history and lives of the people of Glasgow. The Kids Travel Guide to Scotland can guide children through the exhibits, including displays on the city's social history, working-class life, and historical artifacts. Children can learn about the city's past, explore the Winter Gardens' tropical plant collection, and enjoy interactive displays that showcase Glasgow's vibrant culture.

Glasgow Green:

Glasgow Green is the oldest public park in the city and offers ample space for children to play and relax. The Kids Travel Guide to Scotland can highlight the park's attractions, such as the iconic Doulton Fountain and the McLennan Arch. Children can enjoy a picnic on the green, play in the playgrounds, or rent bicycles to explore the park's extensive paths. Glasgow Green also hosts various events and festivals throughout the year, providing additional entertainment and cultural experiences.

Street Art and Murals:

With countless murals gracing the city's walls, Glasgow is renowned for its thriving street art culture. The Kids Travel Guide to Scotland can highlight some of the notable murals and street art locations, such as the famous mural of the "Rangers' 9 in a Row" near Ibrox Stadium. Children can take a walking tour to discover these colorful artworks, learn about the artists behind them, and appreciate the creativity and expression found in Glasgow's streets.

The Tall Ship:

The Tall Ship at Riverside is a unique attraction that allows children to step aboard a fully restored sailing ship. The Kids Travel Guide to Scotland can introduce children to the history of the ship, explaining its role as a cargo vessel in the past. Children can explore the ship's decks, learn about life on board a sailing vessel, and imagine themselves as sailors navigating the high seas.

Scottish Football Museum:

For young sports enthusiasts, the Scottish Football Museum at Hampden Park offers a chance to delve into the rich history of Scottish football. The Kids Travel Guide to Scotland can highlight the museum's exhibits, including iconic football memorabilia and interactive displays. Children can learn about legendary players, important matches, and the passion for football in Scotland. They can even test their skills in interactive games and challenges.

Encourage children to embrace the spirit of exploration as they venture through Glasgow with the Kids Travel Guide to Scotland. Let them take the lead in choosing attractions and activities that capture their interest, allowing them to immerse themselves in the city's art, history, and cultural heritage. Glasgow offers a dynamic and diverse range of experiences that will create lasting memories of their Scottish journey.

Inverness

Inverness, the capital city of the Scottish Highlands, is a charming and picturesque destination that offers a unique experience for young travelers. The Kids Travel Guide to Scotland can serve as an excellent resource to help children discover the wonders of Inverness. Here's a detailed explanation of what children can experience while exploring the city:

Inverness Castle:

Inverness Castle is a prominent landmark that overlooks the city and the River Ness. The Kids Travel Guide to Scotland can introduce children to the castle's history and significance. Although the castle is currently used as a courthouse and not open to the public, children can still admire its impressive exterior and learn about its medieval roots. Encourage children to take a walk along the castle grounds and enjoy the views of the city and the river.

Culloden Battlefield:

The Kids Travel Guide to Scotland can introduce children to the historic Culloden Battlefield, located a short distance from Inverness. Children can learn about the Battle of Culloden, which took place in 1746 and marked the end of the Jacobite Rising. They can explore the battlefield, visit the visitor center, and gain a deeper understanding of this significant event in Scottish history.

Encourage children to reflect on the bravery and sacrifice of those involved in the battle.

Inverness Museum and Art Gallery:

The Inverness Museum and Art Gallery offers children an opportunity to learn about the history, culture, and heritage of the Highlands. The Kids Travel Guide to Scotland can highlight the museum's exhibits, which include artifacts, interactive displays, and artwork. Children can explore topics such as Highland life, archaeology, and natural history. They can also participate in educational workshops and activities that engage their curiosity and creativity.

Whin Park and Ness Islands:

Whin Park and Ness Islands provide an idyllic setting for children to enjoy outdoor activities and nature. The Kids Travel Guide to Scotland can describe the park's playgrounds, walking trails, and picnic areas. Children can have fun exploring the Ness Islands, connected by footbridges, and discover hidden paths, sculptures, and wildlife along the way. Encourage children to bring along a picnic and spend a relaxing day surrounded by the beauty of nature.

Dolphin Spotting:

The Kids Travel Guide to Scotland can inform children about the opportunity to spot dolphins in the Moray Firth, near Inverness. They can learn about the bottlenose dolphins that inhabit these waters and the best places to observe them, such as Chanonry Point. Children can join a guided dolphin-watching tour or simply keep a lookout from the shore. Encourage them to engage in responsible wildlife observation practices and appreciate the beauty of these magnificent creatures in their natural habitat.

Inverness Botanic Gardens:

The Inverness Botanic Gardens offer children a chance to explore various themed gardens and learn about different plant species. The Kids Travel Guide to Scotland can describe the gardens' features, such as the tropical house, cactus house, and sensory garden. Children can enjoy the colorful displays, learn about the importance of plants, and engage in interactive activities that promote environmental awareness and conservation.

Fairy Glen:

Located a short distancefrom Inverness, the Fairy Glen is a magical and enchanting place that children will love to explore. The Kids Travel Guide to Scotland can describe the Glen's whimsical landscapes, with its small hills, winding paths, and sparkling streams. Children can let their imaginations run wild as they search for fairies, build fairy houses, and discover the hidden nooks and crannies of this mystical location.

Inverness Leisure Centre:

The Inverness Leisure Centre offers a range of activities and facilities for children to enjoy. The Kids Travel Guide to Scotland can highlight the center's swimming pools, ice rink, and sports halls. Children can have fun splashing around in the pools, learning to ice skate, or engaging in various sports and games. The leisure center provides a great opportunity for children to stay active and have fun, especially on rainy days.

Highland Wildlife Park:

A short drive from Inverness, the Highland Wildlife Park is an exciting destination for children to observe and learn about a variety of animals. The Kids Travel Guide to Scotland can describe the park's unique features, including the drive-through safari experience and the opportunity to see native Scottish wildlife such as red deer and Highland cows. Children can also encounter other animals like polar bears, snow leopards, and wolves. They can appreciate the importance of conservation and the beauty of the animal kingdom.

Encourage children to embrace the spirit of adventure as they explore Inverness with the Kids Travel Guide to Scotland. Let them choose the attractions and activities that capture their interest, allowing them to immerse themselves in the city's history, nature, and cultural heritage. Inverness offers a wealth of opportunities for children to learn, have fun, and create lasting memories of their Scottish journey.

CHAPTER 4

Discovering Scottish Nature

Scottish Highlands

The Scottish Highlands are a vast and breathtakingly beautiful region that offers a multitude of adventures for young travelers. The Kids Travel Guide to Scotland can serve as an excellent resource to help children discover the wonders of the Scottish Highlands. Here's a detailed explanation of what children can experience while exploring this enchanting region:

Scenic Landscapes:

The Kids Travel Guide to Scotland can introduce children to the stunning landscapes of the Scottish Highlands. They can learn about the towering mountains, shimmering lochs (lakes), cascading waterfalls, and picturesque valleys that define the region. Encourage children to appreciate the natural beauty of the Highlands as they embark on scenic drives, hikes, or boat trips to explore the diverse and awe-inspiring landscapes.

Wildlife Watching:

The Scottish Highlands are home to a rich array of wildlife. The Kids Travel Guide to Scotland can describe the various animals children may encounter, such as red deer, Highland cows (coos), otters, eagles, and puffins (in coastal areas). Children can engage in wildlife spotting activities and learn about the importance of preserving these creatures and their habitats. Encourage them to keep a watchful eye and respect the wildlife from a safe distance.

Castles and Ruins:

The Scottish Highlands are dotted with historic castles and ruins that provide a glimpse into the region's rich history. The Kids Travel Guide to Scotland can introduce children to iconic castles such as Eilean Donan Castle, Urquhart Castle, and Dunrobin Castle. They can learn about the castles' pasts, explore their grounds, and even imagine themselves as knights or princesses. Ruined castles, such as Castle Urquhart on the shores of Loch Ness, offer an opportunity for children to immerse themselves in history and let their imaginations run wild.

Jacobite Steam Train:

The Kids Travel Guide to Scotland can highlight the Jacobite Steam Train, also known as the Hogwarts Express from the Harry Potter films. Children can embark on a magical journey through the Scottish Highlands, crossing the famous Glenfinnan Viaduct

[53]

and passing through stunning landscapes. The train ride offers a memorable and enchanting experience, evoking a sense of wonder and adventure.

Fairy Pools and Folklore:

The Kids Travel Guide to Scotland can transport children to the Fairy Pools on the Isle of Skye, where crystal-clear pools and waterfalls create a magical setting. They can learn about the folklore and legends associated with fairies and mythical creatures. Encourage children to let their imaginations soar as they explore these enchanting landscapes and create their own stories inspired by the beauty of the Fairy Pools.

Nature Trails and Hiking:

The Kids Travel Guide to Scotland can guide children through nature trails and hikes suitable for their age and abilitiesin the Scottish Highlands. They can discover scenic trails that lead to breathtaking viewpoints, waterfalls, and hidden gems. Children can learn about the importance of respecting nature, following marked paths, and leaving no trace. Encourage them to engage their senses and appreciate the sights, sounds, and scents of the Highland wilderness.

Dark Sky Reserves:

The Scottish Highlands are home to Dark Sky Reserves, areas with minimal light pollution that offer incredible stargazing opportunities. The Kids Travel Guide to Scotland can introduce children to the wonders of the night sky and the importance of protecting dark skies. They can learn about constellations, planets, and the possibility of seeing shooting stars. Encourage children to venture out on clear nights, armed with blankets and a sense of wonder, to gaze up at the vast expanse of the universe.

Highland Folk Museum:

The Highland Folk Museum provides a unique opportunity for children to step back in time and experience Scottish Highland life from centuries ago. The Kids Travel Guide to Scotland can describe the museum's exhibits, which include traditional buildings, artifacts, and interactive demonstrations. Children can engage in hands-on activities, try on period costumes, and learn about the customs and traditions of the Highlands' past inhabitants.

Encourage children to embrace the spirit of adventure and discovery as they explore the Scottish Highlands with the Kids Travel Guide to Scotland. Let them immerse themselves in the region's natural wonders, history, and folklore. The Scottish Highlands offer a magical and unforgettable experience that will create lasting memories of their Scottish journey.

Lochs and Islands

Scotland is renowned for its stunning lochs (lakes) and picturesque islands, which provide a wealth of opportunities for young travelers to explore and enjoy. The Kids Travel Guide to Scotland can serve as an excellent resource to help children discover the wonders of Scotland's lochs and islands. Here's a detailed explanation of what children can experience while exploring these enchanting locations:

Loch Lomond:

Loch Lomond, located in the southern part of the Scottish Highlands, is one of Scotland's most iconic lochs. The Kids Travel Guide to Scotland can introduce children to the beauty of Loch Lomond, with its sparkling waters and surrounding hills. They can learn about the diverse wildlife that inhabits the area, such as otters, birds, and fish. Children can enjoy boat rides on the loch, go fishing, or embark on leisurely walks along its shores.

Isle of Skye:

The Kids Travel Guide to Scotland can transport children to the magical Isle of Skye, located on the west coast of Scotland. They can learn about the island's stunning landscapes, including the famous Fairy Pools, the Old Man of Storr rock formation, and the

[56]

dramatic Cuillin Mountains. Children can immerse themselves in the island's enchanting folklore and explore its rugged beauty through hikes, wildlife spotting, and visits to historic sites such as Dunvegan Castle.

Loch Ness:

No exploration of Scotland's lochs would be complete without delving into the mysteries of Loch Ness. The Kids Travel Guide to Scotland can captivate children's imaginations with tales of the legendary Loch Ness Monster, Nessie. They can learn about the history, folklore, and scientific investigations surrounding this famous creature. Children can visit the Loch Ness Centre & Exhibition to discover more about Nessie and enjoy boat tours on the loch in search of the elusive creature.

Isle of Mull:

The Isle of Mull, located on Scotland's west coast, offers a diverse range of attractions for young travelers. The Kids Travel Guide to Scotland can introduce children to the island's wildlife, such as puffins, seals, and eagles. They can explore the colorful waterfront town of Tobermory, known for its vibrant buildings and lively harbor. Children can also visit the famous Duart Castle, perched on a cliff overlooking the sea, and learn about the island's rich history and culture.

[57]

Loch Tay:

The Kids Travel Guide to Scotland can guide children to Loch Tay, a picturesque loch in the central Highlands. They can learn about the loch's history and legends, including the story of the Iron Age Crannog, a reconstructed ancient dwelling. Children can enjoy outdoor activities such as kayaking, fishing, and cycling around the loch. They can also visit the Scottish Crannog Centre to learn more about life in ancient Scotland.

Orkney Islands:

The Kids Travel Guide to Scotland can transport children to the captivating Orkney Islands, located off the northeastern coast of Scotland. They can learn about the islands' rich archaeological heritage, including the UNESCO World Heritage Sites of Skara Brae and the Ring of Brodgar. Children can explore ancient ruins, discover Neolithic tombs, and learn about Viking history through interactive exhibits. They can also enjoy the islands' rugged landscapes, stunning beaches, and diverse birdlife.

Loch Katrine:

Loch Katrine, located in the heart of the Trossachs National Park, is a tranquil and scenic loch that inspired the famous poem "The Lady of the Lake" by Sir Walter Scott. The Kids Travel Guide to Scotland can introduce children to the beauty of Loch Katrine,

[58]

surrounded by mountains and forests. They can take a boat trip on the loch, cycle along its shores,or embark on walks through the surrounding countryside. Children can learn about the history and wildlife of the area, including the native red deer and ospreys that inhabit the region.

Isle of Arran:

The Isle of Arran, often referred to as "Scotland in Miniature," offers a diverse range of landscapes and attractions for children to explore. The Kids Travel Guide to Scotland can introduce children to the island's stunning scenery, including rugged mountains, sandy beaches, and rolling farmland. They can visit Brodick Castle and Gardens, learn about the island's wildlife at the Arran Heritage Museum, or enjoy outdoor activities such as hiking and cycling. Children can also indulge in the island's renowned ice cream and locally produced food.

Loch Awe:

Loch Awe, one of Scotland's longest lochs, is nestled in the beautiful Argyll and Bute region. The Kids Travel Guide to Scotland can describe the loch's scenic surroundings, with ancient forests, mountains, and historic castles. Children can visit Kilchurn Castle, a ruined fortress set on a peninsula, and learn about its intriguing history. They can also enjoy fishing, boating, or simply exploring the loch's shoreline and nearby walking trails.

Shetland Islands:

The Kids Travel Guide to Scotland can take children on an adventure to the Shetland Islands, located northeast of the Scottish mainland. They can learn about the islands' unique culture, including the annual Up Helly Aa fire festival and the traditional Shetland pony. Children can explore the dramatic cliffs, sandy beaches, and archaeological sites that dot the islands. They may also have the chance to spot seals, puffins, and other wildlife along the rugged coastline.

Highland Cows

Highland cows, also known as Highland cattle or "coos," are an iconic breed of cattle native to Scotland. These shaggy-haired creatures are a popular attraction for visitors, especially children, who are captivated by their unique appearance and gentle nature. The Kids Travel Guide to Scotland can introduce children to the charm and characteristics of Highland cows. Here's a detailed explanation of what children can learn about these beloved animals:

Appearance:

The Kids Travel Guide to Scotland can describe the distinctive appearance of Highland cows, which sets them apart from other cattle breeds. Children can learn about their long, shaggy hair that varies in colors such as red, black, or brindle. They can observe the cow's impressive set of horns, which both males and females possess. Children may notice that their long hair serves as protection against the harsh Scottish weather, keeping them warm in cold winters and offering shade in the summer.

Personality and Temperament:

Highland cows are known for their calm and docile nature, making them an ideal breed for children to observe and interact with. The Kids Travel Guide to Scotland can highlight the gentle temperament of Highland cows, explaining that they are generally friendly and non-aggressive. Children can learn about the importance of respecting the cows' personal space and approaching them with caution. Encourage children to appreciate the quiet nature of these animals and observe their behavior from a safe distance.

Role in Scottish Culture:

The Kids Travel Guide to Scotland can educate children about the historical and cultural significance of Highland cows in Scotland. They can learn that these cows have been a part of Scottish

[61]

agriculture and rural life for centuries, providing milk, meat, and hides for various purposes. Highland cows have also become an enduring symbol of Scotland's countryside, appearing in artworks, photographs, and even on souvenirs. Children can understand the cultural pride associated with these unique animals.

Conservation Efforts:

The Kids Travel Guide to Scotland can inform children about the conservation efforts dedicated to preserving the Highland cow breed. They can learn that Highland cows were once endangered, but through conservation programs, their numbers have increased. Children can appreciate the role played by farmers, breeders, and conservation organizations in ensuring the survival of these distinctive animals. They can also understand the importance of biodiversity and the need to protect unique breeds like the Highland cow.

Farm Visits and Interactions:

The Kids Travel Guide to Scotland can encourage children to visit farms and Highland cow habitats, where they can observe these magnificent animals up close. Children may have the opportunity to meet and interact with Highland cows, under the supervision of farmers or tour guides. They can learn about the cows' diet, how they are cared for, and the role they play in sustainable farming practices. Visiting a farm allows children to develop a deeper connection with these gentle creatures and appreciate the vital role they play in Scotland's rural communities.

Highland Cow Crafts and Souvenirs:

Children can get creative and engage in Highland cow-themed arts and crafts projects inspired by their visit to Scotland. The Kids Travel Guide to Scotland can suggest activities such as creating paper or clay Highland cow models, painting pictures, or designing their own Highland cow souvenirs. Children can express their admiration for these animals through their artistic creations and take home a lasting reminder of their experience with Highland cows.

CHAPTER 5

Uncovering Scottish History and Legends

Ancient Scotland

Scotland has a rich and fascinating ancient history that spans thousands of years, encompassing remarkable archaeological sites, ancient monuments, and captivating legends. The Kids Travel Guide to Scotland can serve as an excellent resource to help children explore the wonders of ancient Scotland. Here's a detailed explanation of what children can learn about ancient Scotland:

Stone Circles and Standing Stones:

The Kids Travel Guide to Scotland can introduce children to the ancient stone circles and standing stones that dot the Scottish landscape. They can learn about iconic sites such as the Ring of Brodgar in Orkney, the Callanish Stones on the Isle of Lewis, and the Clava Cairns near Inverness. Children can discover the mysteries surrounding these ancient structures, including their purpose, construction methods, and the legends and rituals associated with them.

Skara Brae:

Skara Brae, located on the Orkney Islands, is a remarkably well-preserved Neolithic village that offers a glimpse into the lives of ancient inhabitants. The Kids Travel Guide to Scotland can transport children back in time as they explore the stone-built houses and learn about the daily lives of the people who lived there over 5,000 years ago. Children can discover the ancient tools, furniture, and artifacts that have been unearthed at the site, gaining an understanding of the Neolithic way of life.

Broch Towers:

Broch towers are ancient stone structures that can be found throughout Scotland, particularly in the northern parts. The Kids Travel Guide to Scotland can explain the purpose of these towers, which served as defensive structures, residences, and symbols of power during the Iron Age. Children can learn about the construction techniques used to build these impressive towers and imagine what life might have been like for the people who lived in them.

Pictish Stones and Symbols:

The Picts were an ancient people who inhabited Scotland during the early medieval period. The Kids Travel Guide to Scotland can introduce children to Pictish stones and symbols, which are intricately carved stones that depict various designs, animals, and symbols. Children can learn about the mysterious Picts and their artistic achievements, and they can try to decipher the meanings behind the symbols carved into the stones.

Castles and Fortifications:

Scotland is renowned for its castles and fortifications, many of which have ancient origins. The Kids Travel Guide to Scotland can highlight notable examples such as Edinburgh Castle, Stirling Castle, and Dunnottar Castle. Children can learn about the history of these structures, the people who built them, and the roles they played in Scotland's ancient past. They can explore the castle grounds, visit the impressive interiors, and imagine themselves as knights or princesses from ancient times.

Celtic Mythology and Legends:

The Kids Travel Guide to Scotland can introduce children to the captivating world of Celtic mythology and legends. They can learn about ancient Scottish folklore, including stories of mythical creatures like the Loch Ness Monster, selkies (seal people), and kelpies (water spirits). Children can immerse themselves in the tales of heroes, fairies, and gods, gaining insight into the beliefs and imagination of ancient Scotland.

Celtic Crosses and Symbols:

The Kids Travel Guide to Scotland can educate children about Celtic crosses and symbols that are prevalent in Scottish art and heritage. They can learn about the intricate designs and symbolism behind these ancient symbols, such as the Celtic knotwork, spirals, and animals. Children can appreciate the beauty of Celtic artwork and understand the cultural significance of these symbols in Scottish history.

Ancient Burial Sites:

Scotland is home to ancient burial sites that hold clues about the rituals and beliefs of past civilizations. The Kids Travel Guide to Scotland can introduce children to sites such as the Tomb of the Eagles in Orkneyand the Clava Cairns near Inverness. Children can learn about the practices of burial and commemoration in ancient Scotland, including the construction of tombs, the placement of grave goods, and the rituals associated with honoring the deceased. They can explore these sites, ponder the mysteries of the past, and gain a deeper appreciation for the ancient cultures that once thrived in Scotland.

Iron Age Brochs:

The Kids Travel Guide to Scotland can introduce children to Iron Age brochs, which are circular stone towers found primarily in the northern parts of Scotland. Children can learn about the purpose

[67]

and construction of brochs, which served as fortified homes and defensive structures. They can imagine what life might have been like for the ancient inhabitants, exploring the ruins and gaining insight into the Iron Age way of life.

Viking Influence:

The Viking Age had a significant impact on Scotland's history, and the Kids Travel Guide to Scotland can introduce children to the Viking influence in ancient Scotland. Children can learn about the Norse invaders, their settlements, and their interactions with the local population. They can discover Viking artifacts, hear tales of Viking warriors, and explore the Norse heritage that is still evident in certain areas of Scotland.

Scottish Myths and Legends

Scotland is steeped in myths, legends, and folklore that have been passed down through generations. These captivating stories bring the landscape to life and provide a glimpse into the rich cultural heritage of the country. The Kids Travel Guide to Scotland can serve as an excellent resource to introduce children to the enchanting world of Scottish myths and legends. Here's a detailed explanation of what children can discover:

Loch Ness Monster (Nessie):

The Kids Travel Guide to Scotland can captivate children with the legendary tale of the Loch Ness Monster, affectionately known as Nessie. They can learn about the mysterious creature said to inhabit the depths of Loch Ness and the numerous sightings and stories associated with it. Children can explore the Loch Ness Centre & Exhibition, discover the scientific investigations carried out, and develop their own theories about the existence of Nessie.

Kelpies:

The Kelpies are mythical water spirits that take the form of horses. The Kids Travel Guide to Scotland can introduce children to these captivating creatures of Scottish folklore. They can learn about the tales of the Kelpies luring unsuspecting travelers into water bodies and the importance of respecting the waters. Children can also visit the iconic Kelpies sculptures near Falkirk and marvel at the magnificent representations of these legendary creatures.

Selkies:

Selkies are fanciful creatures with the ability to change from seals into people. The Kids Travel Guide to Scotland can enchant children with stories of selkies and their connection to the sea. They can learn about the tales of selkies shedding their seal skins to roam the land as humans and the themes of love and longing that often accompany these legends. Children can let their imaginations soar as they ponder the possibility of encountering a selkie on the Scottish coastline.

Brownies:

Brownies are helpful and mischievous creatures from Scottish folklore. The Kids Travel Guide to Scotland can introduce children to these friendly household spirits. They can learn about the tales of brownies completing household chores and the importance of showing gratitude and kindness to these little beings. Children can embrace the idea of a mischievous brownie friend who may assist them during their adventures in Scotland.

Fairy Folklore:

The fairy folklore of Scotland is rich and varied, with tales of magical beings inhabiting the landscape. The Kids Travel Guide to Scotland can immerse children in the world of fairies and introduce them to different types of fairies found in Scottish folklore, such as the "seelie" and "unseelie" fairies. Children can learn about the customs and beliefs surrounding fairies, including leaving offerings in fairy glens and respecting their habitats. They can let their imaginations run wild as they explore locations associated with fairies, such as Fairy Glen on the Isle of Skye.

The Blue Men of the Minch:

The waters of the Minch, a body of water between the Hebrides and the mainland, are thought to be home to the fabled beings known as the Blue Men of the Minch. The Kids Travel Guide to Scotland can spark children's curiosity about these intriguing beings. They can learn about the tales of the Blue Men causing storms, singing haunting songs, and interacting with sailors. Children can ponder the mysteries of the deep sea and imagine encounters with these mystical creatures.

The Fairy Pools of Skye:

The Kids Travel Guide to Scotland can transport children to the enchanting Fairy Pools on the Isle of Skye. They can learn about the magical reputation of these natural pools, surrounded by stunning waterfalls and surrounded by beautiful landscapes. Children can immerse themselves in the legends and tales associated with the Fairy Pools, imagining the presence of fairies and magical creatures as they explore this captivating location.

The Stone of Destiny:

The Stone ofDestiny, also known as the Stone of Scone, is an ancient symbol of Scottish kingship. The Kids Travel Guide to Scotland can introduce children to the legends and historical significance of this stone. They can learn about the tales of kings being crowned upon the Stone of Destiny and its connection to

[71]

Scottish sovereignty. Children can visit Edinburgh Castle and see the Stone of Destiny on display, allowing them to appreciate its place in Scotland's history.

The Green Lady of Stirling Castle:

The Green Lady is a ghostly figure said to haunt Stirling Castle. The Kids Travel Guide to Scotland can intrigue children with the story of the Green Lady and the legends surrounding her. They can learn about the tales of her appearance and the possible reasons for her ghostly presence. Children can visit Stirling Castle and explore the rooms where the Green Lady is said to have been sighted, fostering their fascination with Scotland's haunted history.

The Legend of Braveheart:

The Kids Travel Guide to Scotland can introduce children to the legendary figure of William Wallace, known as Braveheart. They can learn about his role in Scotland's fight for independence and the iconic battles he led against English rule. Children can visit sites associated with William Wallace, such as Stirling Bridge, and imagine the courage and determination he displayed in his quest for freedom.

CHAPTER 6

Scottish Traditions and Festivals

Tartan and Kilts

Tartan and kilts are iconic symbols of Scottish culture and heritage, representing the traditional dress of Scotland. The Kids Travel Guide to Scotland can introduce children to the fascinating world of tartan and kilts. Here's a detailed explanation of what children can learn about these important aspects of Scottish identity:

Tartan:

The Kids Travel Guide to Scotland can explain that tartan is a distinct pattern of crisscrossed horizontal and vertical bands of colors. Each tartan is associated with a specific clan, family, or region in Scotland. Children can learn that tartan has a long history and was traditionally used to identify and differentiate Scottish clans and families. They can explore the rich variety of tartan patterns and colors, each with its unique significance and symbolism.

Clan Tartans:

The Kids Travel Guide to Scotland can introduce children to the concept of clan tartans. They can learn that tartans were historically associated with specific Scottish clans, representing their family heritage and identity. Children can discover their own clan tartan if they have Scottish ancestry, or they can learn about the tartans of famous Scottish clans such as Macdonald, Campbell, or MacLeod. They can appreciate the sense of belonging and pride that comes with wearing their clan's tartan.

Regional Tartans:

In addition to clan tartans, there are also regional tartans that represent specific areas of Scotland. The Kids Travel Guide to Scotland can highlight regional tartans such as the Black Watch tartan for the Highlands or the Royal Stewart tartan for the royal family. Children can learn about the historical and cultural significance of these regional tartans and how they are still used today in various contexts.

Kilt:

The Kids Travel Guide to Scotland can explain that a kilt is a traditional Scottish garment that is made from tartan fabric. Children can learn that a kilt is a pleated, knee-length skirt-like garment that is typically worn by men in formal and ceremonial settings. They can explore the different components of a kilt, including the tartan pattern, the sporran (a pouch worn at the front), the belt and buckle, and the kilt pin. Children can appreciate the craftsmanship and symbolism behind the kilt.

Dressing in a Kilt:

The Kids Travel Guide to Scotland can provide a step-by-step guide for children on how to dress in a kilt. They can learn how to properly wear and fasten a kilt, ensuring that the pleats are positioned correctly and the accessories are appropriately styled. Children can understand the importance of wearing a kilt with pride and respect for Scottish tradition and culture.

Modern Usage:

While tartan and kilts have deep historical roots, they are still relevant in modern Scottish culture. The Kids Travel Guide to Scotland can explain that tartan is used in a variety of ways beyond traditional clothing, such as home decor, accessories, and even corporate branding. Children can discover the versatility of tartan and its enduring presence in contemporary Scottish society.

Tartan and Identity:

The Kids Travel Guide to Scotland can foster children's understanding of how tartan and kilts are symbols of Scottish identity. They can learn that wearing tartan or a kilt can signify a connection to Scottish heritage and a sense of pride in one's roots. Children can appreciate how tartan and kilts serve as visual representations of Scotland's rich cultural heritage and can be worn to celebrate Scottish events and traditions.

Highland Games

The Highland Games are a vibrant and exciting part of Scottish culture, showcasing traditional sports, music, and festivities. The Kids Travel Guide to Scotland can introduce children to the thrill and spectacle of the Highland Games. Here's a detailed explanation of what children can learn about these unique events:

History and Origins:

The Kids Travel Guide to Scotland can delve into the history and origins of the Highland Games. Children can learn that the Games date back centuries and were originally organized as a way to test the strength, skill, and agility of Scottish clansmen. They can understand that the Games have evolved into a celebration of Scottish culture and a gathering that fosters community spirit and friendly competition.

Events and Competitions:

The Kids Travel Guide to Scotland can describe the various events and competitions that take place during the Highland Games.

Children can learn about traditional sports such as the caber toss, where participants flip a large log, and the hammer throw, where athletes launch a metal ball attached to a handle. They can also discover other events like tug-of-war, stone putting, and the famous Highland dancing competitions. Children can imagine themselves participating in these exciting challenges and engaging in friendly rivalry.

Music and Dance:

The Kids Travel Guide to Scotland can introduce children to the lively music and dance performances at the Highland Games. They can learn about traditional Scottish music, including bagpipe melodies and lively fiddle tunes. Children can discover the art of Highland dancing, characterized by intricate footwork, energetic movements, and colorful costumes. They can appreciate the rhythms and melodies that accompany the Games, immersing themselves in the vibrant atmosphere.

Traditional Dress:

The Kids Travel Guide to Scotland can explain the significance of traditional dress at the Highland Games. Children can learn about the kilt, tartan patterns, and other elements of Scottish attire. They can understand that participants and attendees often wear kilts, sporrans (pouches), and other accessories, adding to the festive and cultural ambiance. Children can appreciate the beauty and symbolism of traditional Scottish dress and perhaps even have the opportunity to try on a kilt themselves.

Community and Culture:

The Kids Travel Guide to Scotland can emphasize the sense of community and cultural pride fostered by the Highland Games. Children can learn that the Games bring people together from different backgrounds to celebrate Scottish traditions. They can understand the importance of preserving Scottish culture and heritage through events like the Highland Games. Children can appreciate the camaraderie and sportsmanship displayed during the Games, as participants and spectators come together in a spirit of unity and friendly competition.

Children's Activities:

The Kids Travel Guide to Scotland can highlight the special activities and events tailored for children at the Highland Games. Children can participate in mini versions of traditional events, such as sack races, mini caber toss, or welly throwing. They can enjoy face painting, storytelling, and other interactive experiences that allow them to engage with Scottish culture. Children can experience the excitement and joy of the Highland Games in a way that is age-appropriate and tailored to their interests.

[79]

Hogmanay (New Year's Eve) Celebrations

Hogmanay is the Scottish term for New Year's Eve, and it is a time of vibrant celebrations and cherished traditions. The Kids Travel Guide to Scotland can introduce children to the excitement and festivities of Hogmanay. Here's a detailed explanation of what children can learn about this special occasion:

The Meaning of Hogmanay:

The Kids Travel Guide to Scotland can explain the significance of Hogmanay in Scottish culture. Children can learn that Hogmanay is a time to bid farewell to the old year and welcome in the new year with joy and enthusiasm. They can understand that it is a time for family, friends, and communities to come together and celebrate the turning of the year.

Torchlight Processions:

One of the iconic features of Hogmanay celebrations is the torchlight procession. The Kids Travel Guide to Scotland can describe the spectacle of thousands of people marching through the streets with lit torches, creating a mesmerizing and magical atmosphere. Children can learn about the history behind this tradition and the symbolism of carrying the torches to ward off evil spirits and bring good luck for the new year.

Fireworks Displays:

Fireworks are a highlight of Hogmanay celebrations, illuminating the night sky with brilliant colors and sparkling lights. The Kids Travel Guide to Scotland can introduce children to the excitement of fireworks displays that take place in cities and towns across Scotland. Children can learn about the dazzling visual spectacle and the tradition of fireworks symbolizing a fresh start and a bright future.

First-Footing:

First-Footing is a beloved Hogmanay tradition where the first person to enter a home after midnight brings good luck for the coming year. The Kids Travel Guide to Scotland can explain the customs associated with First-Footing, such as carrying a lump of coal, a piece of bread, or a bottle of whisky as gifts for the household. Children can learn about the warm welcome extended to the first-footer and the significance of sharing hospitality and goodwill.

Ceilidhs and Music:

Ceilidhs are lively gatherings where people come together to enjoy traditional Scottish music, dancing, and merriment. The Kids Travel Guide to Scotland can introduce children to the joyous atmosphere of ceilidhs during Hogmanay. They can learn about traditional Scottish music instruments, such as the bagpipes, fiddles, and drums, and discover the energetic dances like the Scottish reel. Children can appreciate the sense of community and celebration that permeates the ceilidh experience.

New Year's Resolutions:

The Kids Travel Guide to Scotland can explain the concept of New Year's resolutions, where people make promises to themselves for self-improvement in the coming year. Children can learn about the idea of setting goals and aspirations for the future, such as being kinder, learning new skills, or pursuing hobbies. They can reflect on their own resolutions and the opportunities that a new year brings.

Loony Dook:

The Loony Dook is a playful and exhilarating tradition that takes place on New Year's Day. The Kids Travel Guide to Scotland can describe the Loony Dook, where participants dress in wacky costumes and plunge into icy waters, such as rivers or the sea. Children can learn about the spirit of fun and bravery behind this event and understand that it symbolizes letting go of the past and embracing the challenges of the new year with a fresh start.

The Edinburgh Festival Fringe

The Edinburgh Festival Fringe is the largest arts festival in the world and a highlight of Scotland's cultural calendar. The Kids Travel Guide to Scotland can introduce children to the vibrant and creative atmosphere of the Edinburgh Festival Fringe. Here's a detailed explanation of what children can learn about this extraordinary event:

What is the Edinburgh Festival Fringe?

The Kids Travel Guide to Scotland can explain that the Edinburgh Festival Fringe is an annual arts festival that takes place in Edinburgh, the capital city of Scotland. Children can learn that it is a celebration of performing arts, including theater, comedy, music, dance, and more. They can understand that the Fringe is open to all artists and performers, from amateurs to professionals, providing a platform for creativity and expression.

History and Origins:

The Kids Travel Guide to Scotland can delve into the history and origins of the Edinburgh Festival Fringe. Children can learn that it began in 1947 as an alternative event running alongside the Edinburgh International Festival. They can understand that the Fringe quickly grew in popularity, becoming a unique and diverse festival that celebrates artistic innovation and freedom of expression.

Performances and Shows:

The Kids Travel Guide to Scotland can showcase the wide range of performances and shows that take place during the Edinburgh Festival Fringe. Children can learn about the incredible variety of acts, from theater plays and musical performances to stand-up comedy, street performances, and circus acts. They can explore the program of events, highlighting shows suitable for families and children of different ages.

Street Performances:

Street performances are an integral part of the Edinburgh Festival Fringe. The Kids Travel Guide to Scotland can introduce children to the joy and excitement of watching street performers in action. They can learn that artists take to the streets and public spaces, showcasing their talents and captivating audiences with their skills and creativity. Children can appreciate the spontaneous and interactive nature of street performances, creating memorable experiences for all.

Children's Shows and Activities:

The Kids Travel Guide to Scotland can emphasize the special shows and activities designed specifically for children during the Edinburgh Festival Fringe. Children can discover a wide array of performances tailored to their age group, including puppetry, storytelling, magic shows, and interactive theater experiences. They can participate in workshops, creative activities, and special events designed to engage their imaginations and nurture their love for the arts.

Exploring the Fringe:

The Kids Travel Guide to Scotland can provide tips and suggestions for exploring the Edinburgh Festival Fringe with children. Children can learn about the different venues, including theaters, pop-up stages, and outdoor spaces, where performances take place. They can understand the concept of purchasing tickets in advance or taking advantage of free shows and street performances. Children can also learn about the vibrant atmosphere of the Fringe's main hub, the Royal Mile, where artists and performers gather to promote their shows.

Street Food and Festive Atmosphere:

The Edinburgh Festival Fringe offers more than just performances. The Kids Travel Guide to Scotland can highlight the lively street food stalls, where children can sample a variety of delicious treats and snacks from different cuisines. They can soak in the festive atmosphere of street performers, musicians, and crowds of people celebrating the arts. Children can appreciate the sense of community and joy that permeates the Fringe.

CHAPTER 7

Tasting Scotland

Traditional Scottish Food

Scotland is known for its rich culinary heritage, and the Kids Travel Guide to Scotland can introduce children to the flavors and traditions of traditional Scottish food. Here's a detailed explanation of what children can learn about the delightful world of Scottish cuisine:

Scottish Breakfast:

The Kids Travel Guide to Scotland can start by introducing children to the hearty Scottish breakfast. They can learn that it typically includes items such as bacon, eggs, sausages, black pudding (a type of blood sausage), baked beans, mushrooms, and tattie scones (potato pancakes). Children can discover the importance of starting the day with a filling meal to fuel their adventures.

Haggis:

Haggis is one of Scotland's most famous traditional dishes. The Kids Travel Guide to Scotland can explain that haggis is a savory pudding made from sheep's offal (heart, liver, and lungs), mixed with oats, onions, spices, and suet, all encased in a sheep's stomach. Children can learn about the cultural significance of haggis and the traditional Burns Supper, where haggis is served with neeps (mashed turnips) and tatties (mashed potatoes) during celebrations of poet Robert Burns.

Fish and Chips:

Fish and chips is a beloved dish in Scotland, just like in other parts of the UK. The Kids Travel Guide to Scotland can introduce children to this classic meal, featuring a battered and fried fish fillet served with chunky chips (French fries). Children can learn about the importance of using fresh fish, such as haddock or cod, and the tradition of enjoying this delicious meal wrapped in newspaper.

Scotch Broth:

The Kids Travel Guide to Scotland can highlight Scotch broth, a traditional Scottish soup. Children can learn that Scotch broth is made with lamb or mutton, barley, root vegetables (such as carrots, onions, and turnips), and sometimes pulses like peas or lentils. They can discover the comforting flavors and nourishing qualities of this hearty soup, perfect for colder days.

Shortbread:

Shortbread is a sweet treat that children can discover in the Kids Travel Guide to Scotland. They can learn that shortbread is a buttery, crumbly biscuit made with simple ingredients such as butter, sugar, and flour. Children can appreciate the melt-in-your-mouth texture and the delicious simplicity of this traditional Scottish biscuit.

Cranachan:

Cranachan is a traditional Scottish dessert that showcases some of Scotland's finest ingredients. The Kids Travel Guide to Scotland can explain that cranachan is made with whipped cream, toasted oats, raspberries, and a drizzle of honey or whisky. Children can learn about the combination of flavors and textures in this delightful dessert, and they can appreciate the use of local produce, **such as raspberries from Scottish fields.**

Tattie Soup:

Tattie soup, or potato soup, is a comforting and nourishing dish commonly enjoyed in Scotland. The Kids Travel Guide to Scotland can introduce children to this simple soup made with potatoes, onions, vegetables, and sometimes meat or stock. Children can learn about the versatility of tattie soup, with variations that can include carrots, leeks, or even a hint of spice.

Tablet:

Tablet is a sweet confection that children can discover in the Kids Travel Guide to Scotland. They can learn that tablet is similar to fudge but with a crumbly texture and a rich, sweet flavor. Children can appreciate the indulgence of this treat, often made with sugar, condensed milk, butter, and vanilla.

Trying Scottish Whisky (for the parents!)

Scotland is renowned for its whisky, often referred to as the "water of life." While this topic is more suitable for parents than children, the Kids Travel Guide to Scotland can provide a brief overview of Scottish whisky and its cultural significance. Here's a detailed explanation for parents interested in exploring Scottish whisky:

Scotch Whisky:

The Kids Travel Guide to Scotland can introduce parents to Scotch whisky, which is a specific type of whisky produced in Scotland. They may find out that Scotch whisky is created from malted barley, water, and yeast and is matured for a minimum of three years in oak barrels. The skill and commitment that go into creating this trademark spirit are evident to parents.

Distillery Tours:

The Kids Travel Guide to Scotland can highlight the opportunity for parents to visit whisky distilleries and take guided tours.

Parents can learn about the whisky-making process, from malting and mashing to fermentation and distillation. They can explore the distillery grounds, see the copper stills, and even sample different whiskies, gaining insight into the flavors and nuances that make each whisky unique.

Whisky Tastings:

Parents can engage in whisky tastings during their visit to Scotland. The Kids Travel Guide to Scotland can suggest reputable establishments, such as whisky bars or dedicated whisky tasting experiences, where parents can sample a range of Scotch whiskies. They can learn about the different regions of whisky production in Scotland, each offering distinct characteristics, such as the smoky whiskies of Islay or the fruity notes of the Speyside region.

Appreciating the Flavors:

The Kids Travel Guide to Scotland can explain to parents the art of appreciating the flavors and aromas of whisky. Parents can learn about the importance of nosing (smelling) the whisky, identifying different scents such as vanilla, caramel, or peat smoke. They can also discover the proper technique for tasting, allowing the flavors to unfold on their palate and savoring the complexities of the whisky.

Responsible Enjoyment:

The Kids Travel Guide to Scotland can emphasize the importance of responsible enjoyment when it comes to trying Scottish whisky. Parents can understand the need to drink in moderation and be aware of their limits. They can also learn about the legal drinking age and the significance of drinking responsibly while setting a positive example for their children.

Non-Alcoholic Alternatives:

While parents may indulge in Scottish whisky, it's important to note that Scotland offers a range of non-alcoholic alternatives as well. The Kids Travel Guide to Scotland can suggest parents explore traditional Scottish beverages such as Scottish soda, locally produced juices, or Scottish-themed mocktails. This way, parents can still experience the unique flavors of Scotland without consuming alcohol.

Encourage parents to embrace the opportunity to explore Scottish whisky and its rich heritage while practicing responsible enjoyment. The Kids Travel Guide to Scotland can serve as a starting point for parents to learn about the craftsmanship, traditions, and cultural significance of Scottish whisky, allowing them to immerse themselves in this renowned aspect of Scotland's identity.

[93]

CHAPTER 8

Fun Activities for Kids

Scotland offers a wide range of fun and engaging activities for kids, allowing them to explore the country's natural beauty, history, and cultural heritage. The Kids Travel Guide to Scotland can introduce children to exciting experiences and memorable adventures. Here's a detailed explanation of some fun activities for kids to enjoy in Scotland:

Castle Exploration:

Scotland is home to numerous majestic castles that ignite children's imagination. The Kids Travel Guide to Scotland can highlight castles such as Edinburgh Castle, Stirling Castle, or Dunnottar Castle. Children can embark on castle tours, learn about medieval history, and imagine themselves as knights or princesses. They can explore the castle grounds, discover hidden chambers, and learn about the stories and legends associated with these historic fortresses.

Nature Walks and Hiking:

Scotland's breathtaking landscapes provide endless opportunities for kids to connect with nature. The Kids Travel Guide to Scotland can suggest family-friendly nature walks and hikes suitable for children of different ages and abilities. Children can discover lush forests, sparkling lochs, and rolling hills as they explore trails such as the Fairy Pools on the Isle of Skye or the Trossachs National Park. They can engage in scavenger hunts, identify flora and fauna, and appreciate the beauty of the natural world.

Wildlife Watching:

Scotland is home to an array of fascinating wildlife, and kids can have fun spotting and learning about these creatures. The Kids Travel Guide to Scotland can introduce children to the possibility of encountering animals like red deer, Highland cows, puffins, seals, and dolphins. They can visit wildlife reserves, take boat trips, or even go on guided tours where they can observe and appreciate Scotland's diverse animal kingdom.

Outdoor Adventures:

The Kids Travel Guide to Scotland can inspire children with thrilling outdoor adventures. They can try their hand at activities like kayaking, canoeing, or paddleboarding on Scotland's rivers and lochs. Children can also experience the excitement of cycling or horseback riding in scenic locations such as the Cairngorms National Park or the Isle of Arran. These activities allow children to embrace the spirit of adventure while appreciating Scotland's natural beauty.

Museum Visits:

Scotland's museums offer engaging and interactive experiences for children. The Kids Travel Guide to Scotland can highlight museums such as the National Museum of Scotland, the Museum of Childhood, or the Kelvingrove Art Gallery and Museum. Children can explore exhibits on topics like Scottish history, science, art, and culture. They can participate in hands-on activities, interactive displays, and educational workshops that cater to their curiosity and creativity.

Storytelling and Mythology:

Scotland is rich in myths, legends, and storytelling traditions. The Kids Travel Guide to Scotland can encourage children to immerse themselves in Scottish folklore and mythology. They can visit storytelling centers or attend storytelling events where they can listen to captivating tales of heroes, fairies, and mythical creatures. Children can also engage in creative activities like writing their own stories or performing in impromptu storytelling sessions.

Traditional Crafts:

The Kids Travel Guide to Scotland can introduce children to traditional Scottish crafts and arts. Children can learn about activities like tartan weaving, pottery making, or even creating their own miniature Loch Ness Monster figurines. They can participate in workshops or visit craft centers where they can try their hand at these traditional crafts, learning about Scotland's heritage and developing their artistic skills.

Interactive Exhibits:

Scotland offers interactive exhibits that cater specifically to children's interests. The Kids Travel Guide to Scotland can suggest attractions like Camera Obscura and World of Illusions in Edinburgh, where children can engage with optical illusions, mind-bending puzzles, and interactive displays.

CHAPTER 9

Helpful Phrases and Glossary

The Kids Travel Guide to Scotland can provide children with a list of helpful phrases and a glossary of commonly used words and expressions. This can help them navigate Scotland with ease and engage with locals. Here's a detailed explanation of how children can benefit from learning these helpful phrases and vocabulary:

Greetings:

Children can learn basic greetings to start conversations and show politeness. The Kids Travel Guide to Scotland can teach children phrases like "Hello" (Ciamar a tha thu?), "Goodbye" (Mar sin leibh), and "Thank you" (Tapadh leat). These simple greetings and expressions of gratitude can foster positive interactions with locals.

Introductions:

The Kids Travel Guide to Scotland can provide children with phrases to introduce themselves and make new friends. Children can learn how to say their name (Is mise [name]), ask others for their names (Dè an t-ainm a th'ort?), and exchange simple pleasantries like "Nice to meet you" (Tha e math a bhith a' cluich còmhla riut).

[98]

Asking for Help:

In unfamiliar surroundings, children may need to ask for assistance. The Kids Travel Guide to Scotland can teach children phrases like "Excuse me" (Thoir dhomh leisgeul), "Can you help me?" (Am faigh thu cuideachadh?), or "I'm lost" (Tha mi air chall). These phrases can help children seek guidance or directions if needed.

Ordering Food:

When dining out, children can use basic phrases to order food and drinks. The Kids Travel Guide to Scotland can teach children how to say "I would like..." (Bu toil leam...), "Please" (Ma 's e do thoil e), and names of popular Scottish dishes like "Fish and chips" or "Haggis." This allows children to actively participate in the dining experience and communicate their preferences.

Basic Numbers:

Children can learn basic numbers in Scottish Gaelic to understand prices, count items, or tell the time. The Kids Travel Guide to Scotland can teach children numbers from one to ten, allowing them to communicate simple numerical information.

Common Words and Phrases:

The Kids Travel Guide to Scotland can provide a glossary of common words and phrases children may encounter during their visit. This can include words like "castle" (caisteal), "mountain" (beinn), "loch" (loch), or phrases like "I don't understand" (Chan eil mi a' tuigsinn). Understanding these terms can enhance children's comprehension of their surroundings and enable them to engage more fully with Scottish culture.

Encourage children to practice these phrases and vocabulary with the Kids Travel Guide to Scotland. Let them understand that attempting to speak the local language shows respect and can lead to more meaningful interactions during their visit.

CONCLUSION

In conclusion, Scotland is a land filled with enchantment and wonder, just waiting to be explored by adventurous young hearts. From its majestic castles and mythical creatures to its breathtaking landscapes and vibrant traditions, Scotland offers a truly magical experience for kids of all ages. So pack your bags, embrace the spirit of adventure, and let Scotland's rich history and natural beauty inspire you to embark on an unforgettable journey. Whether you're scaling towering mountains, unraveling ancient mysteries, or dancing to the rhythm of lively ceilidhs, Scotland will captivate your imagination and leave you with cherished memories that will last a lifetime. So go forth, young explorers, and discover the magic that awaits you in bonny Scotland!